PHOENIX POETS

A SERIES EDITED BY TOM SLEIGH

HOLIDAY

SUSAN HAHN

THE UNIVERSITY OF CHICAGO PRESS
Chicago and London

SUSAN HAHN is the editor of *TriQuarterly* magazine and
coeditor of TriQuarterly Books. She is the author of three
books of poems: *Harriet Rubin's Mother's Wooden Hand* (1991);
Incontinence (1993), which won the Society of Midland
Authors poetry award; and *Confession* (1997), all published
by the University of Chicago Press.

The University of Chicago Press, Chicago 60637
The University of Chicago Press, Ltd., London
© 2001 by The University of Chicago
All rights reserved. Published 2001
Printed in the United States of America

10 09 08 07 06 05 04 03 02 01   1 2 3 4 5

ISBN: 0-226-31275-5 (cloth)
ISBN: 0-226-31276-3 (paper)

Library of Congress Cataloging-in-Publication Data

Hahn, Susan.
    Holiday / Susan Hahn.
        p.   cm.—(Phoenix poets)
    ISBN 0-226-31275-5 (cloth : acid-free paper)
    ISBN 0-226-31276-3 (paper : acid-free paper)
    I. Title   II. Series
    PS3558.A3238 H65 2001
    811'.54—dc21
                                    2001000766

For Fred and Rick

To Tom

And as the boat-head wound along
The willowing hills and fields among,
They heard her singing her last song. . . .

— TENNYSON, "THE LADY OF SHALLOT"

Contents

SURCEASE

Acknowledgments

Grateful acknowledgment is made to the editors of publications in which these poems, or versions of them, first appeared:

Boulevard: "Swan Song of the Sad Woman at the Birth of the Millennium," fall 2000

Chelsea: "Jail Fever," "The Woman Who Hated Valentine's Day," vol. 70, no. 71, summer 2001

Michigan Quarterly Review: "Holiday—Part VIII," "The Woman Who Hated New Year's Eve," summer 2001

New England Review: "The Woman Who Loved Halloween," vol. 21, no. 4

Poetry: "Anthem," July 2000; "Her Purse, at the Winter Solstice," December 2000

"Anthem" received *Poetry* magazine's George Kent Prize.

*

With much gratitude to Randolph Petilos

BAGGAGE

The Woman Who Loved Halloween

She's given up the huge
festivals—the bonfires on
the hilltops, the days when the devil's
help was evoked
for health and luck—the twisted
world a tumble down
the tenured land. She's given

up the trick or treat—
the carved out grin of the night watchman.
O how she misses him:
his long bones, his skeleton
heart that she tried to glue
flesh on, his hand
movements—*flexion, extension,*
abduction, adduction; ADDICTION
to the pelvis girdle—
that deep cavity, the flared-
up ilium, the drop
to the pubis that she worshiped on

an autumn evening not unlike this one.
All Hallows' Eve. *Eve* of the dried out
garden, *what is there left to tend?*
Eve, who walks the earth with her jack-
o'-lantern—neither in hell nor in heaven.

The Woman Who Hated
Thanks, Giving

Sad floral cups of cultivated
yeses and *of courses,* too
bright bursts of giving
up, double-layered petticoat of pet-
als—so fragile—with a soft
stem of *thank you, thank you so*
very much. Thanks
for the taking. THE YANK.

O to grow a wild rose that turns
its back to fence and trellis. *NO,*
it shouts in its thorny voice—
NO to *thanks, NO* to *give*—
no give account or give over.

Just itself a rambling gift
to any careful observer.
Thank you whisper the timid flock
for this isolated shock of color,
while it stays silent,
giving thanks to only one—
the golden complement of the sun.

The Woman Who Was Confused by Christmas

Because the birth took place in a closed womb
never to be opened, because the sealed
fountain brought forth water and the unplanted
garden sprung flowers, the world became

a jumbled place of explanations that were not
understandable. Symbols could not be
lacquered to anything
concrete and she longed for the super glue

of some childhood, where there was
a mother and a father and no one entered
from an upper room through bolted doors
or emerged from a locked sepulcher.

True, she also longed for miracles
but only those when the unusual
seemed good for her—then how easily
she blessed what others called delusional.

The Woman Who Hated New Year's Eve

Because her body lies transverse
inside the old year, it can't birth
itself. It needs the help of forceps
to grab her head and press
more deformity into it.
Because she doesn't understand how

to divide up time
(Does the day begin at midnight, dawn?)
she can't count the intervals
between contractions or hold on to her
possessives, especially the state of being

curve. Because she doesn't know
how to go into the dilation
of morning, only the fetal positions of mourning,
she can't take the chance
of pushing out chin first, forcing
her face into the future,

further and further extending herself from her
chest—cage that covers
the bleeding heart. She risks

asphyxiation as horns blow *new*
from other mouths—and kisses, too.

Her Purse, at the Winter Solstice

The needled red tea roses were distorted
by the quilt in the fabric of the cheap cotton
bag she carried through the filth
of snow to the transfusions

and back again to her bed
where she fanned herself
into the soft pink blankets and then closed
into them like a small item,
lost. Sometimes I couldn't find her—

a swansdown powder puff,
misplaced. All night

I'd dream of black taffeta, locked inside
a day bag of white painted metal plaques
or an evening clutch of lacquered brass,
covered with ash, ribbed silk. Her purse

had too deep a background,
where blossoms were pinned down
—stitch to stitch—
with never a hope they could climb off
and into the coming spring air, join

the others. I'd dream of a framed
French carryall, pale blue silk
and silver thread worked into
a pattern of a spiderweb, finished

with a tassel of carved steel
beads, my fingers constantly being cut
by handles decorated with flowered urns
and the cold heads of the sphinxes.

The Woman Who Hated Valentine's Day

A quiver of arrows, a quiver of eros,
she cannot hold bow or beau—
both intent on a massacre
of the heart where each obliterates
the other—nothing left to stitch up.
Catgut has become as weak
as lace. Martyred

Saints beatified and canonized—
it's they whom she idealizes,
as she repeats the rites of purity, the right
tasks. Desperate Psyche on her knees

attempting to serve the myth—
Venus, Please, she cries,
I need to find Him—meaning

Cupid. Instead, in the bent and the dead
forest, the archdemons await:
Lucifer, Mammon, Asmodeus,
Satan, Beelzebub, Leviathan
are tempting her, again.

The Woman Who Became All Ash

After Ash Wednesday

Because her self became all tinder—
dried powder bark that began deep
within her heart, then spread
throughout—she ignited easily.
All spark, all passion, too much—
she turned to anger and then to all
heat and light and after-
ward to the irreducible
extract of ash, the divine living
energy of her fire

departed. Purged, purified, destroyed,
volatilized, punished, sublimated,
her essence was extracted. All manifold
functions creative and negating left
for others to consider as hierophantic

powers. With her they marked
their faces, sprinkled their heads,
covered their bodies. And she,
the white glow residue,

the lust-filled yogins
called the ashes of their semen.

The Woman Who Couldn't Be Good or Right

After Good Friday

Perhaps if she could touch
the relic of the true cross
as if she were a bishop
or a pilgrim nun,
she'd understand the splendid hymns,

the priority of right before
good, or is it good
before right? She cannot
get it straight.
Plato and Aristotle

agreed the contemplative life
was best. She's a hedonist,
but mostly in her fantasies.
Days and nights she sits
in a chair, imagining
the garden, the foliage, the passion-

flower—its five white sepals,
its five white petals
that symbolize the ten apostles,
its purple fringe inside, a crown
of thorns or a halo,
the stamens, wounds,
the styles, nails.
She's dug

sores into her smooth thighs
as she delves for salvation.
Awaits deliverance like the others
in the upheaval of these hours.

The Twisted Girl of Mid-April

No party for her, no fancy
hats or horns to blow—impossible—
her bent neck stiff and fallen
over her right shoulder.
Like any other day—

no holiday—the woman wheels her palsy
into the raging high-
noon sun which hangs there
as if in its own spastic paralysis,
until a rapidly rotating column—
all flex and muscle—forms

underneath a cloud
and a funnel descends
from the suddenly darkened sky
and the twisted girl of mid-April

is pushed inside.
The woman undresses her
and places her in
bed in her still-fetal
position that she's given

up trying to straighten.
And while hail hits

the windows, she imagines being
a flower born into this unpredictable

weather—one that thrives
on warmth and air that's full,
of the hum
of insects and birds
that so casually fly.
This is the unbroken creation

of the birthday girl of mid-April.

The Woman Whose Mother Became "The" Moth

After Mother's Day

In a place where wars and weather
don't wreck lives, only the wasps
who lay their eggs on or in
moth caterpillars—feed
on their fluids—kill.
In a better world

it's the silk from the cocoon—
a single long thread
like a strand of her young hair,
not yet split—that is woven
into beautiful fabric.
The "The"—unstressed,

worn-down case or derivative
from the stem of THAT—is necessary,
yet mostly ignored, buried—
little agile bone. *Remember*
"The" way she lifted
"The" water glass and took her final sip

of this world. Being breaking
free from its hard shell.
"THE" MOTH HER

in question: the objective
case of SHE. *"Please, No More
Semantics or Dramatics."* OK.
Yet, just notice
how certain flowers bloom
in the pitch dark, depend
(O how they depend)
on the night-flying
moth for creation,

how the grains of pollen
swell my pen at 3:00 A.M.

Shame

After Memorial Day

The world doesn't need another poet writing
about memories of her sad wars,
yet in her room she writes on,
mumbling *right on*—
the politics of her private
victories and losses over vague life
and vaguer death.
Listen to the stories of old men:
their deals now buried
six feet under—the monied plots,
power moves, sexual grooves hollowed
by the easy wind. Here, the statues
are strewn with nameless

flowers honoring those who fought to give
the *"I"* its grist. The grease of it
so thick on the lips.
It's a barbeque
to celebrate the skewering
of all enemies—the passing
of the charcoaled chicken wings.
The short men in their shorter shorts joke

and the thin-calved women nibble on
their salad thoughts—
garden of delights so fresh—
while next door a voyeur
peers out, then in, and a gun

goes off. If we're lucky it's just the poet—
pen run out, weapon in mouth.

The Woman Who Prayed to Separate Herself from Memory

After Memorial Day

Amnesia of thoughts a perfect antidote—
the dream of no longer wandering in
retention's confusions. With dis-
use the memory trace—connection
of the synaptic dots—decays
to a clarity. *Just see*
the even jagged teeth of the leaves.
Forget the romance of talk that charges
and recharges hope. Good-bye
to reminiscence. Pray to Aphasia.

Pray to Confabulation—
live in the life one has not—
sweet gooey god of fantasy.
Our rowboat on Lake Como.
Your arms so muscular.
My dress so language fluid.
No bruises to breasts here, no
accusations of "reproach"—your favorite
word. The spit in it allows the tongue

such suppleness, a twist around the stick
like a snake binding itself to a lolli-
pop. All wars

over. The small red
poppies are artificial
and sold only on corners
by disabled veterans. That's all.
THAT'S TOO MUCH. All that's left

is an eidetic image that's quick
to drift off, then resurrect itself at unexpected
moments—necrobiosis of the heart,
until somatic death sets in
and the body temperature drops
to that of its surroundings.
The ice in your voice. The rigor
mortis of what was.
The blood settles
in the low areas of the flesh—
reddish-purple, never to turn back
to the depressed and frightened yellow.

Evolution

After Father's Day

How many ejaculations did it take
to get me—heavy and sunk
to the bottom of the stream?
I lay there so long after

Marduk carved the carcass
of the slain dragon-goddess
and out of it fashioned
heaven and earth and I

followed the stars as they extended
outward and wondered how large
their domain, the sun lying
in its eccentric position—the dust and gas

clouds making the atmosphere so fuzzy
as to what was beyond my galaxy.
Small egg that I was,
envisaging expanding, contracting

oscillating universes. The tilt
of the earth's axis slanted

as best it could toward the light.
It was the longest day, the shortest night,

though in my half-formed, half-thump
of a heart it was continuously dark.
I'd already sensed each murky
day began at midnight with no vision

of what was on either side of life. I yearned
for a placenta, my mother's blood.
She'd not yet been born, or gone—
buried in her red suit,

a Doppler effect—drifting
further away, that color growing
bolder and me left
with the lowercase

father, in the evolution
to human, the daughter cell
with the two X's
looking like cancellations

marking her girl existence,
determined by him.

Anthem

After the Fourth of July

On this night of the mid-
summer festival of fire,
where liquid explosives
look like the arch and ache
of the willow tree

so near your grave, on this
night of the awaiting mid-
wife who lulled you in-
to this world, the light
all violet because the earth and stars
inclined toward each other,
she also sleeps, she who was
your first deliverer, guiding you out

of your mother—her bluing
skin no small sign of the future
cyanosis of her spirit for no
small journey was it to this
country to bring you to birth
in this torch

song heat and an anthem of a free
nation's conception of combustions:
rosins, petroleum, tallow, arsenic
and worse, as you, too, fell from the sky

of her body with me
a microscopic egg inside—
half the composition
that made up my own
toss and tumble to this crash
of ground I sit over and bless
while you lie under, under
the willow, under this world
that no midwife
nor wavelength can under-
standably reach. So I stand

in this over-
determined fire forced out
like bullets upon a target—
the pulled trigger releasing
the hammer that strikes
the impacted mixture—
hailstorm and hymn

of memories. And the outstretched womb
involutes and the abdominal wall tightens
and inside all abandoned encasements
the night over the day darkens.

Jail Fever

After Bastille Day

As it grew hotter
and the July impatiens grew wilder
and the sun splattered the too blue air
with explosive light, a mutiny

occurred on my side of the wire
mesh because I could not touch
the one who would not visit.
I could not reach him. I could
only find myself lost
to his machine-voice
or I was shot,
if he were talking to another,
into voicemail.
And I could not be penitent.
And I could not stay
in my cell without breaking

into a screaming litany:
Sing Sing, San Quentin, Alcatraz
and an echolalia of all that jazz

filled my ears that he had
played for me

two years before in his infected
Bohemia. We danced as high noon hit
the sky and I could not
handle it—the way
his heart branded, his hands raged.
Yet in this fortress

that I've built,
an empty spoon bangs my empty heart
and no savior will come
to storm this cage.

TRIP

Holiday

I

All summer I searched for the holi-
day—a day when the breeze edged
toward a decided quiet and the Sabbath
candles were lit at twilight for just
me and a woman
recited the blessing and kissed the sacred
ache atop my head
and my head did not split
from the spit of news out of the TV set. All summer

the guns shot and the planes dropped and the earth
with its own tender crust and broken
depth threw itself up and the bodies
that twisted in it to stay whole were ripped apart.
And no prayer shawl could cover
any of it—the feet of the dead

always sticking out, reminders that the mind
does not know how to rest over
death. So I lit candles in the heat and incense filled
my room—the pure vanilla smell of innocence
against my incense—that decaying odor
the disillusioned take on. The century had begun
its twist into itself and some of us were losing

our skin—not to rise again. I watched
the Ouroboros happen and lived for the moment
when the snake was so naked and unprotected—
no thick scales to weigh itself
down on the world.
And at the very end of vulnerability

when the overheated flowers could burst
nothing more forth, I yearned for you
to come toward me once more—
to make the fade of our hours
into a love story—a Holiday.

II

Two years today, the princess went
on a holiday. The sun high-
lighted her golden crown, yet by evening
she was melded into the wreckage

of her life. Everyone
wept, but didn't
know exactly why.
Was it the pastels
she wore so well—
how she tried to seduce
the indomitable sky,
challenge every wild
rose to a duel?
In her presence the clouds
seemed mere puffs—
unhappiness, easily dismissed.
Still, that fog
inevitably has to hit
the ground—doesn't it? Yet,
for some seconds

in their timeless lives,
gods, both large and small,
do sleep and sleep
with whomever, taking
their own holiday from their rage

against each other, against us.

III

We met between planes,
not the atmospheric kind,
though, of course, that's always a factor
and your kiss "hello" felt almost
like a beam directly
shined on me from the photosphere.
My hair made a perfect crest
(O slice of moon) across my head
covering the star of hair torn out—

hidden gash. Yet all
we talked about were your other
women, whom you had loved and, now,
did not. I barely
spoke and you didn't notice

my plummet into my skull shell.
Then, I heard *Good-bye, So long,*
Ciao, Adieu and I hated you
while you were off

for a holiday that rose beyond
the horizon of my blurred vision.
Now, exposed—raw and bald and untouched
as the festering sun—
unable to wash off the parting
spindrift left from your lips
against my face,
I sit among the clothes so carefully chosen—
tossed about like planets off their orbits.

Any master plan, unmastered—non-
existent, gone.

IV

So is this how it ends—
or begins? I don't know.
Is the dilation complete
of what comes out, what goes
in? How holy is the day
when the pen is lifted
or put down? Too many question
marks, I think, and then I think

again of the amniotic fluid that surrounds
the world: birth of the head,
birth of the shoulders, birth of the torso,
birth of the legs, feet. *What a burden*
to present oneself—to be present
or be absent. That part as yet not lived—
that absolute deadness

of being dead. LIFELONG HOLIDAY
FROM LIFE. My mother asked to be dressed
in a red suit, black leather Mary Janes
with stumpy heels—
Did the morticians include the shoes?
I could barely look at her bald face.—
and my husband wants to wear his best
blue suit, white shirt (not the button down one)
and a somber tie—my choice. His plan
is that he go first, like my father's.
He's still here with a new girlfriend
who knows how to dress in picnic whites.
She's read *Gatsby. Fancy Lady.*
My mother had the plainest

clothes, but we found drawers and drawers filled
with silky gowns. Each night
she'd drift off in such softness,
the opposite of the scratchy wool that encircles
her unembalmed body. The uterus

is a muscular sac, but the contents
quite incompressible
so most of us get out
face first or with our globed heads
directed backward toward the right or
left. *A Birthday. A Holiday.* The time-
table set—the hour, the day, the year and the dash
left hanging there until
we're planted in the earth or ocean or garden
with some indifferent hand recording the end.
Don't worry over this today, I say.
It's Labor Day. A Holiday. Rest

your mind. Think only with your heart—
that rotting stump. After twenty-three months
he sent an e-mail—turn-of-the-century
love letter. He Did.
An invitation for next month.
R.S.V.P. through his secretary. I Did.
Less than six weeks until a holiday
I never thought would again happen.
Forget Death—at least the literal kind,
his love always a physiology
of grand and petit mals.
But, I'll handle it—let my hair grow
in—fill that silver dollar size hole

I tore out because of his silence.
The boatman will not be paid, today.
The moon's so still but still in the sky.
The message has been sent,
do not for this moment labor over it.

V

Instead of forceps to grasp
her fetal head, a vacuum extractor—
a caplike device—was attached
by suction to her scalp
and she was birthed with a hyper-
tenderness, always pulling

at a body part, mostly her
fingers gnawing at the fontanelle,
until it finally shut like the coffin's vault
and then, at the apex
of the formed skull,
her left arm would arc and her hand
would become the snake's mouth
eating its tail—her mind
the end, then the beginning, then the end
of thought. For hours she'd sit, a being
entirely with and by herself—a world

roiling on, devouring itself
until all motion stopped
and she turned—some say—
into rock in her room,
but that wasn't true.
What it was, was

a fixation—the Ouroboros alone,
exhausted from its rage
and the soul restored
to exanimated stone.

VI

Blown, the twisted horn of submission
at the full moon—the blast
is a weeping: groaning notes
or short wails, all trumpets—
pleas and hopes for inscriptions,
a sweet year in The Book of Life.
The world an apple
dipped in honey. *Bite It.*
This Is Not Eden. But

do not eat a nut,
they produce phlegm and make it more
difficult to recite
the prayers of the day
and, anyway, the numerical value
of the Hebrew for "nut" *(egoz)* is the same
as that for "sin" *(het)*. What rules

to believe in? Who owns
Jerusalem? Mohammed,
who rode the night sky there
to heaven to receive the Koran;
Christ, who walked the Via Dolorosa,
his cross so heavy on his Father's back;
Abraham, who just stood there with tiny Isaac?
How are the Prophets able to sleep

on the Mount of Olives? Do they not hear
the shofar tonight, the bombs
being constructed in the next room?
All sounds fill the temple and drift west
to my mother's grave—to all graves.

Twice, now, this holiday has arrived
without her—woman of quiet and lenience
gone on what is

this noisy Day of Judgement.

VII

i

Nothing was separated out—not the yolk
from the white—the sun from the moon.
All was locked together in a blind shell.
Yet, within the bald darkness there was no rest—
without any long-haired vision to believe in, nothing
to sit down with and comb through, no face
looked in or past the looking glass—
no reflection to reflect upon—a craving
built up and spilt out. God began
to imagine how He might be seen
and a vain, audacious light was born.

ii

And He let his hair grow and though
still short it arched and He
divided it with some spit
on His index finger and thumb—
made a part which ran through
His brain and His mind and His liquid thoughts
split and a creation and prophesy
of divisions began—soon
man from woman, brother from brother and so on. . . .
But for now, it was just
water from water and what He called
heaven and in the mirror of Himself He
smiled at that which was *good* and it was
then He should have stopped.

iii

Soon His hair was long enough to knot
and that is how the earth came about—
around His fingers He twisted it
and spun the waters—His sweat.
In all that motion
the dry land tangled, grew wild—
grass and seeds were flung—
and the fruit tree was conceived.
And He called it *Good*. The blooms
so beautiful—He plucked a berry,
then a plum, then an apple,
decorated His gnarled hair with them
and He Himself became The Tree.

iv

The sun and moon became His
ideas realized and He felt all light
on His head.
It shot through Him where His scalp
was most revealed—at the cowlick,
that crazy splay of thoughts where the part ends—
and He felt it in His heart
and He became as melancholy
as the moon in its wandering cycle.
And God felt old and God felt young
and God felt incomplete
and started pulling out
His hairs one by one,
especially at night and throughout
the seasons and rotations
both around Him and within Him.
And God felt lonesome.

V

So He created the great whales and the fish
and there was life and movement
and He for a moment
stopped tearing at Himself
and took delight
in the turtle and in the snail
as much as He did
in those with quick killer teeth.
And the birds flew and colors
landed everywhere and swept
away His breath. And without
anyone to warn Him it was
truly *then*, He should have stopped.

vi

But He did not, because a restlessness
had burrowed in and He could not stop
thinking up creatures
that crawled and strutted and hulked
and every moving shape imaginable
began to cover the earth. Yet
His agitation only grew worse
and His hair became a mess of knots
until, from His own image—or a shadow of such—
He created man and from him woman
and gave them dominion over all life
and the sun spilled itself and the stars sprinkled
and the skins of all the animals glistened
and it was so perfect, so beautiful—
too much.

vii

Then, He took a holiday—dipped His loosened
hair in the calm seas, rested, then slept,
while the word *Good* repeated itself
in His stupor for each day He had worked.
GOOD, GOOD, GOOD, GOOD, GOOD, GOOD—
it was, wasn't it? GOOD GOADED GOD
so much that on the eighth day—
His hair matted to His head—He awoke
with a start in a terrible sweat with the shakes
and a fever and a too labored shout
over what He had birthed.

VIII

Now that it is the ninth of Tishri
I bring forth from the gut
all sourless apologies, silence
the fits, the bile hours spent.
Repentant before the gates
of heaven—now open but soon to be shut
for one more year, or eternity.
I prepare

for my fast with too much food,
(fast food—no pun here)
not the brisket, or the latkes,
patiently created in my grandmother's kitchen.
It's *her* day to be busy, busy
feeding family, but she's locked in
a vault today and can't get out
no matter how frantic the urgencies
of her knocks, the power of her fist.
To gain strength

I wear white—starched-out color
of purity and mercy—it constricts
the body, makes it more a supplicant. *Sorry. Sorry*—
say the congregants. *(Sorry. Sorry
is what he said after the hurl
of his body onto me,
but that's another story—his cross
to carry or just chop up
for firewood.)* We are talking to God,

referring back to before
my digression

and after my slip.
(I didn't wear a slip,
just a velvet skirt and soft blouse
atop my pure white underwear.
Easy target for him to point the arrow at.
"Always the victim," he said
that too, with such sarcasm
and out of breath.) But not

today on the ninth of Tishri
when the body *must* be afflicted.
No food or drink after sunset is just
the beginning of the litany of acts against
the self—the *Sorry Sorrys*
are shrouding the rooms,
the streets, the cities.

IX

i

The Plain Weave Prayer

It is the simplest and most common.
Please, it wails to God, *Help Me.*
It is the oldest screaming, screaming
through the ginghams, percales and wools.
Crosswise threads pass through the warp
of the world and an insistent pattern
forever redundant is fashioned, stubborn.

The Twill Weave Prayer

It is so tightly put together,
every row is on the diagonal
like a rage not let out
that causes truth to tilt
and the body to sway. Hands are raised
to fists or prayer. How we twist

toward Him (today) in the temple. *Constantly*
apologizing for what we aren't—can never be.
Our limitation, His creation.
Why did he weave so strong a will
into Himself—a pattern, no matter how
magnifiable, the lenses of our eyes
cannot absorb enough to follow?

The Satin Weave Prayer

So delicate it is in all its refined
beauty that He can almost miss
the quiet fabric of its voice, so busy He is
with the grunts—how they snag His world,
remind Him how unfinished
He is. Yet, sometimes His hand reaches
out and touches the splendor of such cloth—
the rich damask of thought, the innocent radiance
of hope—and He feels quite whole.

X

October 1

(morning)

Mother, two days ago he left
with another woman
for a tour of Jerusalem.
Together they'll visit the Old City,
including Mount Zion and the tunnel
excavations under the Wall; arrive
at the Jewish Quarter and the Citadel Museum;
walk along the Cardo, the underground
Roman street; be driven to the Masada
and ascend the rock fortress where the Zealots
made their last stand, then took their own
lives. *He is not a Zealot, but I*
believe in suicide. Then, they'll swim in the Dead

Sea and enjoy the mud
baths. *It rained here yesterday*
on your grave and the grass over
it was so sparse and soft—the ground
a sponge. If I would have chosen, could I have dug
down to you? Tomorrow or the day after

they go to Mount Nebo, the burial place
of Moses. *How many Commandments
can anyone handle?* Will he think of you
before *that* grave? Those long months
of your dying, when he'd disappear—
was it to be with her? And when he visits

the "rose red city" of Petra—carved
out of solid rock, surrounded by soaring
temples and elaborate tombs—will he
think of the empty red suit that your bones are dressed in—
the healthy fleece covered by an oily
substance that protects the sheep
from the rain, forever dried out?

(afternoon)

I wished him a good trip—was polite—
and can only imagine
what it would be like to be at
Yad Vashem—the memorial to the six million—
and what the synagogue with the Chagall stained
windows might look like when the sun hits
the glass at high noon. *Here, the sun hit*
your plaque, creating a wet, golden maple leaf
effect that you would have liked.
Your favorite season has arrived
without you and he's gone

to Old Jaffa, Tel Aviv, the Diaspora
Museum. Soon, we'll all be scattered
relics beneath the ground, waiting only
for some archeologist to dig up
and examine. *Let him go,*
I said to my hand, my closed palm.
His last trip to the holy
land, that's what he said. A place
I've never been and probably never
will be, my eyes just left to absorb the *angered*

red I see over
and over. Is that the reason—your fury
over dying, *over him*—why you insisted
on a suit of rage, slowly becoming invisible,
outside the margin of what we could possibly see?

(night)

My brain can no longer organize
the nerve signals and my green thoughts
are a jumble—
hardly the complement to what
you are shredded in.
I have stumbled through the spectrum
of emotion—gone full circle
on the wheel, spun
from yellow to orange to purple,
have ground through all the blues
and always come back
from my inward travels to you—
undone by what is done—
to leave only the sun-
flowers on your autumn grave—forever
the honeybee hovering near home
for any hope of pollen.

SURCEASE

Swan Song of the Sad Woman at the Birth of the Millennium

I

Monday's child is fair of face

Because there is no real song of the swan
except what a single heart adorns
with prayers of confession—the vanities
the face presents—the tongue wags
tiresome, yet begins again
with moist lips and the world

a thousand years ago warred over
land and people
traveled on the backs of animals
with whips and in the meadow
a woman gave birth to herself and marveled

at her beauty, her own
image repeated, but soon what seemed so fair
felt unfair, because she knew she was
no longer young and there was nothing
to do but mourn herself

into the ground for the surgeons
with their miniature tools and minute
delays of the death mask
were centuries away.

II

Tuesday's child is full of grace

Because there is no real song of the swan
except what a single heart adorns
with notes of thanks and praise,
a lovely silence beds the tongue and the world

a thousand years ago was more
than a small ornament
of forests and people traveled by foot
and in the meadow a woman gave birth

and no one recorded it and it was quiet
except for the initial scream of the girl
into the whirl of the plush green
and for the life she came to bless

and gracefully abandoned with her death.

III

Wednesday's child is full of woe

Because there is no real song of the swan
except what a single heart adorns
with the weight of wretchedness—
the bite into the bitter
apple that freed death to its wanderlust—
a scum coats the tongue and the world

a thousand years ago traded in people—
power struggles to trump little, a power
struggle to stave off the inevitable—
and in the meadow a woman
gave birth to a monster that was and was not

hers and he was
anointed *Ruler, Emperor, King, God*
and her empty chamber was a collage of decay
with its ivory, its copper, its gold, its slaves.

IV

Thursday's child has far to go

Because there is no real song of the swan
except what a single heart adorns
with the whisper of feathers
to ward off the sound crush of thunder—
that far place the scared tongue
curls away from and the soul
is pulled toward—and the world

a thousand years ago could only count on wood
for heat and light to protect it from the night
of unpredictable weather—
no bombs yet, just the crackle and slam
of the atmosphere—and in the meadow
a woman gave birth to a wanderer

and he left her over and over, always
orbiting farther away as she chased after.

V

Friday's child is loving and giving

Because there is no real song of the swan
except what a single heart adorns
with the hum of the hangman's day—
the soon to be crucified, unknowing,
breaks bread with friends, the executioner
awaits his love—
a suffering cankers the tongue and the world

a thousand years ago was pocked with lesions
from arrows and spears and swords and nails
and suits of ringed mail and pointed helmets
with protective bridges of jutting metal
and in the meadow a woman gave birth
in the confusion of blood and armor

and they called her *goddess, mother, mistress, whore.*

VI

Saturday's child works hard for its living

Because there is no real song of the swan
except what a single heart adorns
with the clink of coins—thin, smooth wafers of hammered high-
grade silver which calm the tongue
of the December ploughman who uses his
fattened oxen like so many machines:
his currency, he'll exchange for the "crazy bread"
of poppies, hemp, darnel, plucked, dried, ground up
to produce a medieval hash—and the world

a thousand years ago filled with the poor
who endured their hunger
with the help of lush, artificial heavens,
while the rich reveled in their own ornate halls
and in the meadow a woman gave birth
to a hero that in her somnolent vertigo
she named Survival.

VII

And a child that's born on the Sabbath day
Is fair and wise and good and gay

Because there is no real song of the swan
except what a single heart adorns
with positive adjectives—bubbles (or spittle)
of light and easy words on the tongue
to celebrate the coming or return
of the Savior—whatever it *is,* is

getting closer as the sun drifts indifferent
to the Sunday Sabbath—commemorative
of the resurrection or midnight cabal
presided over by the devil—
the Sunday sun does not care and the world

a thousand years ago prepared
for this crossroad in time—a Holiday
filled with loose, unbalanced eternal
platitudes of wonders and despairs
and in the meadow a woman is about to
give birth to what she does not know
and fears to meet—Manic—

one minute she believes it will be
fair, wise and good,
the next, she believes she'll just be midwife
to her own mute, torn arrival—
bearing down on the unbearable,
sad end of sound.